Mastering Business Taxes

The Ultimate Guide, Tips, Insights and Strategies For Small Business Owners, LLCs, S-Corps and Sole Proprietors To Maximizing Profits And Minimizing Liability (Book 2).

-- By Louis Coleman --

Text Copyright © by Louis Coleman

All rights reserved. No part of this guide may be reproduced in any form without permission in writing from the publisher except in the case of brief quotations embodied in critical articles or reviews.

Legal & Disclaimer

The information contained in this book and its contents is not designed to replace or take the place of any form of medical or professional advice; and is not meant to replace the need for independent medical, financial, legal or other professional advice or services, as may be required. The content and information in this book have been provided for educational and entertainment purposes only.

The content and information contained in this book have been compiled from sources deemed reliable, and it is accurate to the best of the Author's knowledge, information, and belief. However, the Author cannot guarantee its accuracy and validity and cannot be held liable for any errors and/or omissions. Further, changes are periodically made to this book as and when needed. Where appropriate and/or necessary, you must consult a professional (including but not limited to your doctor, attorney, financial advisor or such other professional advisor) before using any of the suggested remedies, techniques, or information in this book.

Upon using the contents and information contained in this book, you agree to hold harmless the Author from and against any damages, costs, and expenses, including any legal fees potentially resulting from the application of any of the information provided by this book. This disclaimer applies to any loss, damages or injury caused by the use and application, whether directly or indirectly, of any advice or information presented, whether for breach of contract, tort, negligence, personal injury, criminal intent, or under any other cause of action.

You agree to accept all risks of using the information presented inside this book.

You agree that by continuing to read this book, where appropriate and/or necessary, you shall consult a professional (including but not limited to your doctor, attorney, or financial advisor or such other advisor as needed) before using any of the suggested remedies, techniques, or information in this book.

TABLE OF CONTENTS

INTRODUCTION 5
SECTION 1: BUSINESS TAXATION 7
   A COMPREHENSIVE INTRODUCTION TO BUSINESS TAXATION ... 7
   PARTNERSHIPS: UNDERSTANDING TAXATION AND LEGALITIES 11
   LLC VS PARTNERSHIPS: UNDERSTANDING KEY DIFFERENCES AND BENEFITS 15
   CORPORATIONS: UNDERSTANDING THEIR FORMATION, TAXES, AND EFFECTIVE MANAGEMENT 19
   PARTNERSHIP FILING: THE PROCESS WITH CLEAR, STEP-BY-STEP EXAMPLES 23
   PARTNERSHIP BASIS: UNDERSTANDING THE CONCEPT OF HOW TO CALCULATE IT, AND ITS IMPLICATIONS 27
   PARTNERSHIP DISTRIBUTIONS: UNDERSTANDING THE DIFFERENT TYPES, HOW THEY ARE TREATED FOR TAX PURPOSES 31
   S-CORPORATION TAX RETURNS: A DETAILED GUIDE TO FORM 1120S 35
   C-CORPORATION TAX RETURNS: A DETAILED GUIDE TO FORM 1120S (PART 1) 39
   ADVANCED C-CORPORATION FILING: NAVIGATING SPECIAL TAX SITUATIONS (PART 2) 43
SECTION 2: TAXATION LAW 46
   UNDERSTANDING COMMON LAW IN BUSINESS TAXATION 46
   UNDERSTANDING THE UNIFORM COMMERCIAL CODE (UCC) AND ITS APPLICATIONS IN BUSINESS TAXATION 49
   UNDERSTANDING AGENCY LAW IN BUSINESS: KEY CONCEPTS AND APPLICATIONS 53
   UNDERSTANDING BANKRUPTCY LAW IN BUSINESS TAXATION . 57

SECTION 3: SPECIAL TAX SITUATIONS 61
   DEPRECIATION DEMYSTIFIED: BASICS AND TAX CALCULATION METHODS 61
   SECTION 179 EXPLAINED: HOW TO MAXIMIZE ITS TAX BENEFITS FOR YOUR BUSINESS 65
   PROPERTY TRANSACTIONS (1231): WHAT YOU NEED TO KNOW FOR TAX BENEFITS 68
   SPECIAL PROPERTY TRANSACTIONS: A BUSINESS TAX GUIDE 72
CONCLUSION 77
CHECK OUT OTHER BOOKS 79

INTRODUCTION

Welcome to **"Mastering Business Taxes: The Ultimate Guide, Tips, Insights and Strategies for Small Business Owners, LLCs, S-Corps & Sole Proprietors to Maximizing Profits and Minimizing Liability."** In an ever-changing landscape of tax regulations and economic fluctuations, understanding business taxation is more crucial than ever. This guide is designed to demystify the complexities of business taxes and provide you with actionable insights to optimize your tax strategy and enhance your financial performance.

Why Business Taxation Matters

For many business owners, the intricacies of tax laws can be overwhelming. However, having a firm grasp on taxation can be a game-changer. It can mean the difference between a thriving business and one that struggles to stay afloat. Effective tax management not only ensures compliance but also unlocks opportunities for substantial financial savings and operational efficiencies. This book aims to equip you with the knowledge and tools needed to navigate the tax landscape confidently.

What You Will Learn

This comprehensive guide is structured to take you through every aspect of business taxation, from foundational principles to advanced strategies. We begin with a broad overview **in Section 1,** covering the basics of business taxation and diving into specific business structures such as partnerships, LLCs, and corporations. Each chapter provides detailed explanations, practical examples, and step-by-step instructions to help you understand and apply key concepts effectively.

Deep Dive into Taxation Law

In Section 2, we explore the legal frameworks that underpin business taxation. Understanding these laws is essential for making informed decisions and avoiding potential pitfalls. We cover common law principles, the Uniform Commercial Code (UCC), agency law, and bankruptcy law, offering insights into how these areas impact your tax obligations and strategies.

Navigating Special Tax Situations

Section 3 addresses special tax situations that businesses often encounter. We demystify complex topics such as depreciation, Section 179 deductions, and property transactions. This section provides you with the knowledge to maximize tax benefits and make informed decisions about your business assets.

A Practical and Engaging Approach

Throughout this book, we aim to make the content engaging and accessible. Taxation can be a dry and daunting subject, but our goal is to present it in a way that is both informative and interesting. Each chapter is filled with real-world examples, practical tips, and strategies that you can implement immediately. Whether you are a small business owner, an LLC member, or a shareholder in an S-Corp or C-Corp, you will find valuable information tailored to your specific needs.

Your Journey to Mastery

"Mastering Business Taxes" is more than just a guide; it is your companion in the journey towards financial acumen and business success. By the end of this book, you will not only understand the nuances of business taxation but also be equipped to leverage this knowledge for the benefit of your business.

Thank you for embarking on this journey with us. Let's unlock the full potential of your business through effective tax management.

SECTION 1: BUSINESS TAXATION

A COMPREHENSIVE INTRODUCTION TO BUSINESS TAXATION

Introduction:

Navigating the complexities of business taxation is essential for any business owner. Different business structures have different tax implications, and understanding these can help you manage your business more effectively and take advantage of available tax benefits. This chapter will provide a comprehensive introduction to business taxation, explaining the basics of various business structures, their tax obligations, and illustrating key concepts with clear examples.

Types of Business Structures

Business structures significantly impact how taxes are filed and paid. Here are the primary business structures and their tax implications:

1. **Sole Proprietorship**
   - **Description:** A sole proprietorship is a one-person business.
   - **Tax Filing:** Income and expenses are reported on Schedule C (Form 1040).
   - **Liability:** There is no legal separation between the owner's personal and business assets. Personal assets are at risk for business debts.

Example: Sole Proprietorship Tax Filing

Alice owns "Top Tennis," a sole proprietorship. She reports her business income and expenses on Schedule C, attached to her Form 1040. Her total income and expenses are combined with her personal tax return.

2. **General Partnership**
   - **Description:** A general partnership involves two or more people sharing profits and losses.
   - **Tax Filing:** The partnership files Form 1065, and income or loss is passed through to the partners, who report it on their personal tax returns using Schedule K-1.
   - **Liability:** Partners' personal assets are at risk for business debts.

Example: General Partnership Tax Filing

Bill and Bob run a hot dog stand as a general partnership. They file Form 1065, and each receives a Schedule K-1 showing their share of the partnership's income or loss. Bill and Bob report this on their individual tax returns.

3. **C Corporation**
    - **Description:** A C corporation is a separate legal entity from its owners.
    - **Tax Filing:** The corporation files Form 1120, and the income is taxed at the corporate level. Shareholders are taxed on dividends.
    - **Liability:** Owners are protected from personal liability for business debts.

Example: C Corporation Tax Filing

"XYZ Manufacturing Inc." is a C corporation. It files Form 1120 to report its income and pay corporate taxes. Shareholders report dividends received on their personal tax returns.

4. **S Corporation**
    - **Description:** An S corporation is a pass-through entity, meaning income is passed through to shareholders and taxed at their individual rates.
    - **Tax Filing:** The S corporation files Form 1120S, and income or loss is reported on shareholders' Schedule K-1.
    - **Liability:** Owners are protected from personal liability for business debts.

Example: S Corporation Tax Filing

"LMN Consulting Inc." is an S corporation. It files Form 1120S, and each shareholder receives a Schedule K-1 showing their share of the income or loss, which they report on their personal tax returns.

5. **Limited Liability Company (LLC)**
    - **Description:** An LLC can be a single-member (treated as a sole proprietorship) or multi-member (treated as a partnership).

- **Tax Filing:** Single-member LLCs file Schedule C, while multi-member LLCs file Form 1065. LLCs can also elect to be taxed as a corporation.
- **Liability:** Owners are protected from personal liability for business debts.

Example: LLC Tax Filing

"OPQ Services LLC" is a multi-member LLC. It files Form 1065, and each member receives a Schedule K-1 showing their share of the income or loss, which they report on their personal tax returns.

Key Tax Forms and Their Uses

1. **Schedule C (Form 1040):** Used by sole proprietors to report income and expenses.
2. **Form 1065:** Used by partnerships and multi-member LLCs to report income and expenses.
3. **Form 1120:** Used by C corporations to report income and pay corporate taxes.
4. **Form 1120S:** Used by S corporations to report income and pass it through to shareholders.
5. **Schedule K-1:** Issued to partners and S corporation shareholders to report their share of income or loss.

Example: Filling Out Key Tax Forms

Alice's Schedule C:

- **Gross Receipts:** $100,000
- **Expenses:** $40,000
- **Net Profit:** $60,000 (reported on Alice's Form 1040)

Bill and Bob's Form 1065:

- **Total Income:** $200,000
- **Total Expenses:** $120,000
- **Net Income:** $80,000
- **Bill's Schedule K-1:** $40,000 (reported on Bill's Form 1040)

- **Bob's Schedule K-1:** $40,000 (reported on Bob's Form 1040)

Understanding Tax Obligations and Strategies

1. **Quarterly Estimated Taxes:**
    - Required if you expect to owe at least $1,000 in tax for the year after subtracting withholding and refundable credits.
    - Use Form 1040-ES to make payments.
2. **Tax Deductions and Credits:**
    - **Deductions:** Reduce taxable income (e.g., business expenses, depreciation).
    - **Credits:** Reduce tax liability (e.g., small business health care tax credit).

Example: Utilizing Deductions and Credits

Alice's Deductions:

- **Office Supplies:** $2,000
- **Travel Expenses:** $3,000

Bill and Bob's Credits:

- **Small Business Health Care Tax Credit:** $1,000

Conclusion:

Understanding the basics of business taxation is essential for compliance and effective financial management. By knowing the different business structures, key tax forms, and available deductions and credits, you can better manage your business's tax obligations and optimize your tax strategy.

PARTNERSHIPS: UNDERSTANDING TAXATION AND LEGALITIES

Introduction:

Partnerships are a common business structure where two or more individuals share ownership. This chapter will provide a comprehensive guide to understanding partnerships, their tax obligations, and key legal aspects. Using simple language and clear examples, this guide aims to help beginners grasp the essentials of managing and filing taxes for a partnership.

What is a Partnership?

A partnership is a business structure where two or more people agree to share the profits and losses of a business. Partnerships can be informal agreements or formally established entities, each with specific tax and legal implications.

Types of Partnerships

1. **General Partnership (GP)**
    - **Formation:** Informally created without filing with the state.
    - **Liability:** Partners have unlimited liability, meaning their personal assets are at risk.
    - **Taxation:** Not a taxable entity; income is passed through to partners who report it on their personal tax returns.

Example: General Partnership Formation

Bill and Bob decide to start a hot dog stand. They agree to share profits and losses equally. Without filing any formal paperwork, they have formed a general partnership. Both are personally liable for any debts incurred by the business.

2. **Limited Partnership (LP)**
    - **Formation:** Requires filing with the state and a written partnership agreement.
    - **Liability:** Consists of general partners (unlimited liability) and limited partners (liability limited to their investment).
    - **Taxation:** Similar to general partnerships, income is passed through to partners.

Example: Limited Partnership Formation

Susan and John form "SJ Real Estate LP." Susan is a general partner managing the business, and John is a limited partner who invests capital but does not manage the business. John's liability is limited to his investment in the partnership.

3. **Limited Liability Partnership (LLP)**
    - **Formation:** Requires state filing and a partnership agreement.
    - **Liability:** Partners have limited liability, protecting their personal assets from most business debts.
    - **Taxation:** Income is passed through to partners.

Example: Limited Liability Partnership Formation

"Tech Innovators LLP" is formed by three tech professionals. They file the necessary paperwork with the state and create a partnership agreement. Each partner's liability is limited, protecting their personal assets.

Tax Obligations for Partnerships

1. **Form 1065: U.S. Return of Partnership Income**
    - **Purpose:** Used to report the partnership's income, deductions, gains, and losses.
    - **Due Date:** March 15th (or the 15th day of the third month following the end of the partnership's tax year).

Example: Filing Form 1065

"Bill and Bob's Hot Dogs" must file Form 1065 by March 15th to report their business income and expenses for the previous year. They include all relevant financial details, such as total sales and business expenses.

2. **Schedule K-1: Partner's Share of Income, Deductions, Credits, etc.**
    - **Purpose:** Issued to each partner to report their share of the partnership's income and deductions.
    - **Inclusion:** Each partner includes their Schedule K-1 information on their individual tax returns (Form 1040).

Example: Issuing Schedule K-1

After filing Form 1065, "Bill and Bob's Hot Dogs" generates Schedule K-1 for both Bill and Bob. Each Schedule K-1 shows their share of the partnership's income, which they report on their individual tax returns.

Key Legal Aspects of Partnerships

1. **Partnership Agreement**
   - **Importance:** Defines roles, responsibilities, profit-sharing, and procedures for resolving disputes.
   - **Contents:** Should include details about capital contributions, management roles, and procedures for adding or removing partners.

Example: Partnership Agreement Details

In "SJ Real Estate LP," Susan and John create a detailed partnership agreement outlining Susan's management role, John's capital contribution, profit-sharing ratios, and procedures for dissolving the partnership if necessary.

2. **Unlimited Liability in General Partnerships**
   - **Risk:** Partners are personally liable for business debts and legal actions.
   - **Example:** If "Bill and Bob's Hot Dogs" incurs a debt of $10,000, both Bill and Bob are personally responsible for repaying it.

Example: Unlimited Liability

If "Bill and Bob's Hot Dogs" is sued and loses, both partners' personal assets, such as their homes or cars, could be used to satisfy the judgment.

3. **Limited Liability in LLPs and LPs**
   - **Protection:** Partners' personal assets are generally protected from business debts, except for their investments.
   - **Example:** In "Tech Innovators LLP," partners' personal assets are protected from business liabilities, providing peace of mind.

Example: Limited Liability

If "Tech Innovators LLP" faces a lawsuit, only the partnership's assets are at risk, not the personal assets of the individual partners.

Conclusion:

Understanding the intricacies of partnerships, including formation, liability, and taxation, is crucial for successful business management. By following the guidelines and examples provided in this chapter, you can ensure compliance with tax laws and effectively manage your partnership.

LLC VS PARTNERSHIPS: UNDERSTANDING KEY DIFFERENCES AND BENEFITS

Introduction:

Choosing the right business structure is crucial for both operational success and tax efficiency. This chapter will guide you through the key differences between Limited Liability Companies (LLCs) and Partnerships, highlighting their formation, liability, taxation, and other critical aspects. Using simple language and clear examples, this guide aims to help beginners make informed decisions about their business structure.

What is a Partnership?

A partnership is a business structure where two or more people share ownership. Partnerships can be informal agreements or formally established entities, each with specific tax and legal implications.

Types of Partnerships

1. **General Partnership (GP)**
   - **Formation:** Informally created without filing with the state.
   - **Liability:** Partners have unlimited liability, meaning their personal assets are at risk.
   - **Taxation:** Income is passed through to partners who report it on their personal tax returns using Form 1065.

Example: General Partnership

Bill and Bob decide to start a hot dog stand and agree to share profits and losses equally. Without filing any formal paperwork, they have formed a general partnership. Both are personally liable for any debts incurred by the business.

2. **Limited Partnership (LP)**
   - **Formation:** Requires filing with the state and a written partnership agreement.
   - **Liability:** Consists of general partners (unlimited liability) and limited partners (liability limited to their investment).
   - **Taxation:** Income is passed through to partners.

Example: Limited Partnership

Susan and John form "SJ Real Estate LP." Susan is a general partner managing the business, and John is a limited partner who invests capital but does not manage the business. John's liability is limited to his investment in the partnership.

3. **Limited Liability Partnership (LLP)**
    - **Formation:** Requires state filing and a partnership agreement.
    - **Liability:** Partners have limited liability, protecting their personal assets from most business debts.
    - **Taxation:** Income is passed through to partners.

Example: Limited Liability Partnership

"Tech Innovators LLP" is formed by three tech professionals. They file the necessary paperwork with the state and create a partnership agreement. Each partner's liability is limited, protecting their personal assets.

What is an LLC?

A Limited Liability Company (LLC) is a flexible business structure that combines elements of partnerships and corporations. LLCs provide limited liability to their owners, known as members.

Types of LLCs

1. **Single-Member LLC (SMLLC)**
    - **Formation:** Requires state filing and articles of organization.
    - **Liability:** Members have limited liability, protecting their personal assets.
    - **Taxation:** Treated as a disregarded entity, with income reported on the owner's Schedule C (Form 1040).

Example: Single-Member LLC

Alice forms "Alice's Art Studio LLC" as a single-member LLC. She files articles of organization with the state. Alice's personal assets are protected from business liabilities, and she reports business income on her Schedule C.

2. **Multi-Member LLC (MMLLC)**
    - **Formation:** Requires state filing and articles of organization.

- **Liability:** Members have limited liability, protecting their personal assets.
- **Taxation:** Treated as a partnership, with income passed through to members using Form 1065.

Example: Multi-Member LLC

"Creative Designs LLC" is formed by two graphic designers. They file articles of organization with the state. Each member's liability is limited, and the business income is reported on Form 1065 and passed through to their individual tax returns.

Comparing LLCs and Partnerships

1. Formation

- **General Partnership:** Informally created, no state filing required.
- **Limited Partnership (LP):** Requires state filing and a partnership agreement.
- **Limited Liability Partnership (LLP):** Requires state filing and a partnership agreement.
- **LLC:** Requires state filing and articles of organization.

Example: Formation Process

"Bill and Bob's Hot Dogs" (General Partnership) requires no formal paperwork, while "Tech Innovators LLP" and "Alice's Art Studio LLC" require state filings.

2. Liability

- **General Partnership:** Unlimited liability for all partners.
- **Limited Partnership (LP):** General partners have unlimited liability; limited partners have limited liability.
- **Limited Liability Partnership (LLP):** All partners have limited liability.
- **LLC:** Members have limited liability.

Example: Liability Protection

In "SJ Real Estate LP," John's liability is limited to his investment. In "Alice's Art Studio LLC," Alice's personal assets are protected from business liabilities.

3. Taxation

- **General Partnership:** Income passed through to partners (Form 1065).
- **Limited Partnership (LP):** Income passed through to partners (Form 1065).
- **Limited Liability Partnership (LLP):** Income passed through to partners (Form 1065).
- **Single-Member LLC:** Income reported on Schedule C (Form 1040).
- **Multi-Member LLC:** Income passed through to members (Form 1065).

Example: Tax Filing

"Creative Designs LLC" (Multi-Member LLC) files Form 1065 and issues Schedule K-1 to each member. "Alice's Art Studio LLC" (Single-Member LLC) reports income on Schedule C.

4. Flexibility and Management

- **General Partnership:** Informal management, equal decision-making by partners.
- **Limited Partnership (LP):** General partners manage; limited partners typically do not participate.
- **Limited Liability Partnership (LLP):** All partners can manage the business.
- **LLC:** Flexible management structure; can be member-managed or manager-managed.

Example: Management Structure

In "Bill and Bob's Hot Dogs," both partners equally manage the business. In "SJ Real Estate LP," Susan manages the business while John is a passive investor.

Conclusion:

Choosing between an LLC and a partnership depends on your specific business needs, liability concerns, and tax preferences. By understanding the key differences and implications of each structure, you can make an informed decision that best suits your business goals.

CORPORATIONS: UNDERSTANDING THEIR FORMATION, TAXES, AND EFFECTIVE MANAGEMENT

Introduction:

Corporations are one of the most recognized and structured forms of business entities. They offer numerous benefits, including limited liability, ease of capital acquisition, and perpetual existence. This chapter will provide a comprehensive guide to understanding corporations, their formation, taxation, and management, with clear examples to illustrate each concept.

Types of Corporations

There are two primary types of corporations: C Corporations (C Corps) and S Corporations (S Corps). Both types require the filing of Articles of Incorporation with the state, but they differ in terms of taxation, ownership, and management.

1. **C Corporation (C Corp)**
    - **Formation:** Requires filing Articles of Incorporation with the state.
    - **Ownership:** Can have an unlimited number of shareholders.
    - **Taxation:** Subject to double taxation – the corporation pays taxes on its income, and shareholders pay taxes on dividends.
    - **Liability:** Shareholders have limited liability.

Example: Formation of a C Corporation

"Mitsubishi Corp" files its Articles of Incorporation, including the company name, objectives, location, capital structure, and organizational structure. Once approved by the state, Mitsubishi Corp becomes an official C Corporation.

2. **S Corporation (S Corp)**
    - **Formation:** Requires filing Articles of Incorporation and electing S Corporation status with the IRS.
    - **Ownership:** Limited to 100 or fewer shareholders, who must be U.S. residents.

- **Taxation:** Pass-through taxation – income is passed through to shareholders and reported on their personal tax returns, avoiding double taxation.
- **Liability:** Shareholders have limited liability.

Example: Formation of an S Corporation

"XYZ Consulting Inc." files its Articles of Incorporation and elects S Corporation status. With fewer than 100 shareholders, XYZ Consulting enjoys the benefits of pass-through taxation.

Key Characteristics of Corporations

1. **Legal Entity:** Both C Corps and S Corps are separate legal entities from their owners, meaning the corporation itself can enter into contracts, sue, and be sued.
2. **Limited Liability:** Shareholders' personal assets are protected from business debts and liabilities.
3. **Perpetual Existence:** Corporations continue to exist even if ownership changes or shareholders die.
4. **Ease of Transfer:** Shares of the corporation can be easily transferred without affecting the corporation's operations.

Tax Obligations for Corporations

1. **C Corporation Taxation**
   - **Form 1120:** C Corps must file Form 1120, reporting their income, gains, losses, deductions, and credits.
   - **Double Taxation:** The corporation pays taxes on its income, and shareholders pay taxes on dividends received.

Example: C Corporation Tax Filing

"Mitsubishi Corp" reports $1,000,000 in income and $200,000 in expenses on Form 1120. The taxable income is $800,000, and the corporation pays corporate income tax on this amount. If dividends are distributed to shareholders, those dividends are taxed again on shareholders' personal tax returns.

2. **S Corporation Taxation**

- **Form 1120S:** S Corps must file Form 1120S, reporting their income, gains, losses, deductions, and credits.
- **Pass-Through Taxation:** Income is passed through to shareholders and reported on their individual tax returns using Schedule K-1.

Example: S Corporation Tax Filing

"XYZ Consulting Inc." reports $500,000 in income and $100,000 in expenses on Form 1120S. The net income of $400,000 is passed through to shareholders, who report their share on Schedule K-1 and include it on their personal tax returns.

Corporate Governance

1. **Board of Directors:** Responsible for overseeing the corporation's activities, setting policies, and making major decisions. They appoint officers to manage day-to-day operations.
2. **Shareholders:** Own the corporation through shares and have voting rights on major issues, such as electing directors and approving mergers.

Example: Corporate Governance Structure

"Mitsubishi Corp" has a Board of Directors that meets quarterly to set corporate policies and make strategic decisions. Shareholders vote annually to elect board members and approve significant corporate actions.

Rights and Responsibilities of Shareholders

1. **Voting Rights:** Shareholders can vote on significant corporate matters, including electing directors, approving mergers, and amending the Articles of Incorporation.
2. **Dividends:** Shareholders have the right to receive dividends if declared by the Board of Directors.
3. **Limited Liability:** Shareholders are not personally liable for corporate debts, barring exceptional circumstances like fraud or illegal activities.

Example: Shareholder Rights

Shareholders of "XYZ Consulting Inc." vote on the election of directors and approve a proposed merger with another company. They also receive dividends based on the corporation's profits.

Conclusion:

Understanding the intricacies of forming and managing a corporation, along with its tax obligations, is essential for business success. By following the guidelines and examples provided in this chapter, you can ensure compliance with legal and tax requirements and make informed decisions about corporate governance and operations.

PARTNERSHIP FILING: THE PROCESS WITH CLEAR, STEP-BY-STEP EXAMPLES

Introduction:

Filing taxes for a partnership can seem daunting, but understanding the flow of documents and the key forms involved can make the process much more manageable. This chapter will guide you through a real-world example of partnership filing, illustrating the process with clear, step-by-step examples. Using simple language, this guide aims to help beginners grasp the essentials of partnership taxation.

Real-World Example: Benge Burgers

Let's take a look at Benge Burgers, a burger restaurant started by Bob and John. We will explore their partnership tax return using Form 1065 for the year 2016.

Overview of Form 1065

Form 1065 is an informational return filed by partnerships to report their income, deductions, gains, and losses. The income reported on Form 1065 is not taxed at the partnership level but passes through to the individual partners, who report it on their personal tax returns using Schedule K-1.

Step-by-Step Walk-Through of Form 1065

1. **Part I: Income and Deductions**
    - **Gross Receipts or Sales (Line 1):**
        - Benge Burgers reported $310,845 in sales for the year.
    - **Cost of Goods Sold (Line 2):**
        - The cost of goods sold (COGS) was $67,591. This includes the cost of inventory and other direct costs related to producing the burgers.
        - **Calculation of COGS:**
            - Beginning Inventory: $5,439
            - Purchases: $67,000
            - Ending Inventory: $4,848
            - COGS = Beginning Inventory + Purchases - Ending Inventory = $67,591

- **Gross Profit:**
  - Gross Profit = Sales - COGS = $310,845 - $67,591 = $243,254
- **Ordinary Business Income:**
  - Total Deductions: $214,037 (including salaries, rent, utilities, etc.)
  - Ordinary Business Income = Gross Profit - Total Deductions = $243,254 - $214,037 = $29,217

Example: Deductions Breakdown

- **Salaries and Wages:** $29,000
- **Rent:** $18,000
- **Utilities:** $5,000
- **Other Deductions:** $92,843 (including accounting fees, advertising, bank charges, etc.)

Part II: Partner's Share of Income - Schedule K-1

Each partner receives a Schedule K-1, which details their share of the partnership's income, deductions, and credits. For Benge Burgers, Bob and John are equal partners, so they each receive 50% of the ordinary business income.

Example: Bob's Schedule K-1

- **Ordinary Business Income:** $14,609
- **Guaranteed Payments:** $24,000

Example: John's Schedule K-1

- **Ordinary Business Income:** $14,608
- **Guaranteed Payments:** $24,000

Understanding Guaranteed Payments

Guaranteed payments are payments made to partners for services or use of capital, regardless of the partnership's profitability. These payments are reported as income by the receiving partner and as a deduction by the partnership.

Example: Reporting on Individual Tax Returns

Bob and John each report their share of the partnership income on their personal tax returns. Let's see how Bob reports his income:

1. **Schedule E (Form 1040):**
   - **Partnership Income:** $38,609 (includes ordinary business income and guaranteed payments)
   - **Section 179 Deduction:** $750 (deducted from total partnership income)
2. **Form 1040:**
   - **Total Income Reported:** $37,859 (after Section 179 deduction)

Separately Stated Items

Certain items must be separately stated on the partners' tax returns because they have different tax implications. These include interest income, dividends, capital gains, and Section 179 deductions.

Example: Bob's Separately Stated Items

- **Interest Income:** $54 (from partnership investments)
- **Ordinary Dividends:** $125 (from partnership investments in Microsoft)
- **Net Long-Term Capital Gain:** $1,800

These items are reported on Bob's Schedule B (interest and dividends) and Schedule D (capital gains) of his Form 1040.

Reconciling Schedule K and K-1s

Schedule K is a summary of all partners' Schedule K-1s. It reconciles the total amounts reported on Form 1065 with the amounts reported on each partner's K-1.

Example: Schedule K

- **Ordinary Business Income:** $29,217 (total for all partners)
- **Guaranteed Payments:** $48,000 (total for all partners)
- **Interest Income:** $108 (total for all partners)
- **Ordinary Dividends:** $250 (total for all partners)
- **Net Long-Term Capital Gain:** $3,600 (total for all partners)
- **Section 179 Deduction:** $1,500 (total for all partners)

Conclusion:

Understanding the flow of documents and the key forms involved in partnership filing is crucial for accurate and compliant tax reporting. By following the step-by-step example provided, you can gain confidence in managing and filing partnership taxes.

PARTNERSHIP BASIS: UNDERSTANDING THE CONCEPT OF HOW TO CALCULATE IT, AND ITS IMPLICATIONS

Introduction:

Understanding the basis in a partnership is crucial for accurately managing and reporting taxes. The basis determines the amount a partner has invested in the partnership and what they are at risk for. This chapter will guide you through the concept of partnership basis, how to calculate it, and its implications, using simple language and clear examples to make the process understandable for beginners.

What is Partnership Basis?

Partnership basis represents a partner's investment in the partnership, including contributions, share of income, and share of liabilities. It is used to determine the taxable gain or loss when the partner sells their interest in the partnership, the tax treatment of distributions, and the ability to deduct partnership losses.

Difference Between Basis and Capital Account

It is important to distinguish between a partner's basis and their capital account:

- **Capital Account:** Reflects the partner's equity in the partnership, including capital contributions, withdrawals, and share of income and losses.
- **Basis:** Includes the capital account plus the partner's share of partnership liabilities and other adjustments.

Example: Basis vs. Capital Account

Bob has a capital account balance of $11,000, which includes his initial contribution and additional contributions during the year. However, his basis in the partnership is different because it also includes his share of the partnership's liabilities.

Calculating Partnership Basis

1. **Starting Basis:**
    - This is the initial contribution made by the partner to the partnership. For example, if Bob contributes $5,000 in cash, his starting basis is $5,000.

2. **Adjustments to Basis:**
    - **Increases to Basis:**

- **Capital Contributions:** Additional cash or property contributions increase the basis.
- **Share of Income:** The partner's share of the partnership's ordinary income, separately stated items, and tax-exempt income.
  - **Decreases to Basis:**
    - **Distributions:** Withdrawals or distributions decrease the basis.
    - **Share of Losses:** The partner's share of the partnership's losses.
    - **Non-Deductible Expenses:** Expenses that are not deductible for tax purposes.

Example: Calculating Basis for Bob

Let's assume Bob has the following transactions during the year:

- **Starting Basis:** $5,000
- **Capital Contribution:** $1,000
- **Share of Ordinary Income:** $14,609
- **Separately Stated Items:**
  - Interest Income: $54
  - Dividends: $125
  - Net Long-Term Capital Gains: $1,800
- **Section 179 Deduction:** $750
- **Distributions:** None

Calculation:

- **Initial Basis:** $5,000
- **+ Capital Contributions:** $1,000
- **+ Share of Ordinary Income:** $14,609
- **+ Interest Income:** $54
- **+ Dividends:** $125
- **+ Capital Gains:** $1,800

- - Section 179 Deduction: $750
- - Distributions: $0

Ending Basis: 5,000+1,000+14,609+54+125+1,800−750=21,8385,000 + 1,000 + 14,609 + 54 + 125 + 1,800 - 750 = 21,8385,000+1,000+14,609+54+125+1,800−750=21,838

Bob's ending basis in the partnership is $21,838.

Example: Basis Adjustments with Liabilities

Consider a scenario where partners contribute property with attached debt. Partner C contributes property worth $100 with a $30 mortgage.

Partner Basis Adjustments:

- **Partner A:** Contributes $100 cash, assumes $10 of debt.
    - Basis: $100 + $10 = $110
- **Partner B:** Contributes $100 cash, assumes $10 of debt.
    - Basis: $100 + $10 = $110
- **Partner C:** Contributes $100 property (with $30 debt), assumes $10 of debt.
    - Basis: $100 (property) - $30 (debt) + $10 (assumed debt) = $80

Impact of Liabilities on Basis:

When a partner contributes property with a mortgage:

- The mortgage is treated as a distribution to the contributing partner, reducing their basis.
- The debt is then assumed by the partnership and allocated among partners, increasing their basis.

Example: Impact on Basis

Partner C's contribution results in:

- Initial Basis: $100 (property)
-
    - Debt Relief: $30

-
  - Assumed Debt: $10
- **Ending Basis:** $80

Basis Limitation on Losses

Partners can only deduct losses up to their basis in the partnership. Losses exceeding the basis are carried forward and can be deducted in future years when the basis increases.

Example: Loss Limitation

Bob has an ending basis of $21,838. If the partnership incurs a $25,000 loss:

- Bob's share of the loss: $12,500 (assuming equal partnership)
- Deductible Loss: $12,500 (up to the basis of $21,838)
- Excess Loss: None (since the loss is less than the basis)

Conclusion:

Understanding partnership basis is essential for accurately reporting taxes and managing partnership investments. By following the steps and examples provided in this chapter, you can ensure that you correctly calculate and adjust your partnership basis, enabling you to make informed financial decisions and comply with tax regulations.

PARTNERSHIP DISTRIBUTIONS: UNDERSTANDING THE DIFFERENT TYPES, HOW THEY ARE TREATED FOR TAX PURPOSES

Introduction:

Partnership distributions can be a complex area of taxation, but understanding them is crucial for accurately managing your partnership's finances and tax obligations. This chapter will provide a detailed guide to partnership distributions, including the different types, how they are treated for tax purposes, and real-world examples to illustrate each scenario.

Types of Partnership Distributions

1. **Non-Liquidating Distributions:**
    - These occur when a partner receives a distribution but remains a part of the partnership. This can include cash or property.
    - **Example:** Bob receives a cash distribution of $10,000 but retains his interest in the partnership.

2. **Liquidating Distributions:**
    - These occur when a partner completely withdraws from the partnership, terminating their interest.
    - **Example:** Bob sells his entire 50% share in Benge Burgers and leaves the partnership.

Non-Liquidating Distributions

Non-liquidating distributions are common in partnerships and do not generally result in a gain or loss if the distribution is less than the partner's basis in the partnership.

Example: Cash Distribution

Let's consider a scenario where Bob's basis in Benge Burgers is $20,000 before any distributions.

- **Scenario 1: Cash Distribution**
    - **Before Distribution:**
        - Bob's Basis: $20,000
    - **Distribution:** $10,000 cash

- After Distribution:
  - Bob's Basis: $20,000 - $10,000 = $10,000
- **Tax Implications:** No gain or loss is recognized as the cash distribution does not exceed Bob's basis.

Example: Property Distribution

- **Scenario 2: Property Distribution**
  - Before Distribution:
    - Bob's Basis: $20,000
  - **Distribution:** Property with a fair market value (FMV) of $10,000
  - After Distribution:
    - Bob's Basis: $20,000 - $10,000 = $10,000
  - **Tax Implications:** No gain or loss is recognized as the property distribution does not exceed Bob's basis.

Liquidating Distributions

Liquidating distributions occur when a partner exits the partnership and can result in a gain or loss if the distribution differs from the partner's basis.

Example: Cash Liquidating Distribution

Let's consider Bob's basis in Benge Burgers is $20,000 before the liquidation.

- **Scenario 3: Cash Liquidating Distribution**
  - Before Distribution:
    - Bob's Basis: $20,000
  - **Distribution:** $10,000 cash
  - After Distribution:
    - Bob's Basis: $20,000 - $10,000 = $10,000
  - **Tax Implications:** As Bob is leaving the partnership, the remaining basis of $10,000 is recognized as a loss. This loss is reported on Form 1040, Line 14, as an ordinary loss.

Example: Property Liquidating Distribution

- **Scenario 4: Property Liquidating Distribution**
  - **Before Distribution:**
    - Bob's Basis: $20,000
  - **Distribution:** Property with an FMV of $10,000
  - **After Distribution:**
    - Bob's Basis: $20,000 - $10,000 = $10,000
  - **Tax Implications:** No gain or loss is recognized as the property is assigned a basis equal to the partner's remaining basis, thus reducing Bob's basis to zero without recognizing a loss.

Distributions Exceeding Basis

When distributions exceed a partner's basis, they must recognize a gain.

Example: Cash Distribution Exceeding Basis

- **Scenario 5: Distribution Exceeding Basis**
  - **Before Distribution:**
    - Bob's Basis: $5,000
  - **Distribution:** $10,000 cash
  - **After Distribution:**
    - Bob's Basis: $0 (Basis cannot be negative)
  - **Tax Implications:** Bob must recognize a gain of $5,000 (Distribution - Basis). This is reported on Form 1040, Line 14, as an ordinary gain.

Tax Reporting

1. **Form 1065:**
   - Partnerships file Form 1065 to report income, deductions, gains, and losses.
   - Distributions are reported on Line 19.
2. **Schedule K-1:**

- Each partner receives a Schedule K-1, which includes their share of the partnership's income and distributions.
- Non-liquidating and liquidating distributions are included here.

Example: Schedule K-1 Reporting

For Bob's $10,000 cash distribution:

- **Schedule K-1, Box 19:** Shows the distribution received.
- **Form 1040:** Reflects the gain or loss if applicable.

Conclusion: Mastering Partnership Distributions

Understanding the various types of partnership distributions and their tax implications is essential for accurate financial and tax reporting. By following the guidelines and examples provided in this chapter, you can ensure that your partnership distributions are correctly managed and reported.

S-CORPORATION TAX RETURNS: A DETAILED GUIDE TO FORM 1120S

Introduction:

Filing taxes for an S-Corporation can seem complex, but breaking it down into manageable steps can make the process more straightforward. This chapter will provide a detailed walk-through of filing an S-Corporation tax return using Form 1120S, complete with real-world examples to illustrate each step. Our example will focus on "Healthy Cupcakes Inc." to help you understand how to file and what to expect.

Understanding S-Corporations

An S-Corporation (S Corp) is a special type of corporation created through an IRS tax election. S Corps avoid double taxation by passing corporate income, losses, deductions, and credits to shareholders for federal tax purposes. Shareholders of S Corps report the flow-through of income and losses on their personal tax returns and are assessed tax at their individual income tax rates.

Key Characteristics of S-Corporations:

- **Limited Liability:** Shareholders have limited liability for the debts of the business.
- **Pass-Through Taxation:** Avoids double taxation; income flows through to shareholders.
- **Restrictions:** Must have 100 or fewer shareholders, all of whom must be U.S. citizens or residents, and can only have one class of stock.

Filing Requirements

S-Corporations must file Form 1120S annually to report their income, gains, losses, deductions, credits, etc. Additionally, each shareholder must receive a Schedule K-1, which details their share of the corporation's income, deductions, and credits.

Real-World Example: Healthy Cupcakes Inc.

Step 1: Basic Information and Income

1. **Form 1120S - Page 1:**
    - **Name and Address:** Enter "Healthy Cupcakes Inc.", followed by the business address.

- **EIN:** Enter the Employer Identification Number (EIN) of Healthy Cupcakes Inc.
- **Date Incorporated:** January 1, 2015.
- **S Election Effective Date:** January 1, 2016.

2. Income Section:
   - **Line 1a (Gross Receipts or Sales):** $591,331
   - **Line 2 (Cost of Goods Sold):** $222,662
   - **Gross Profit (Line 3):** $591,331 - $222,662 = $368,669

Step 2: Deductions and Taxable Income

1. Deductions:
   - **Line 7 (Compensation of Officers):** $100,000
   - **Line 13 (Salaries and Wages):** $80,000
   - **Line 16a (Depreciation):** $12,000
   - **Line 19 (Other Deductions):** $75,629
   - **Total Deductions:** $267,629

2. Taxable Income:
   - **Ordinary Business Income (Line 21):** $368,669 - $267,629 = $101,040
   - **Net Income (Line 22):** $101,040

Step 3: Schedule K-1 Preparation

1. Shareholder Information:
   - **Shareholder:** Mark Hunt
   - **Ownership Percentage:** 100%
   - **Share of Ordinary Business Income:** $101,040

2. Schedule K-1:
   - **Box 1 (Ordinary Business Income):** $101,040
   - **Box 2 (Interest Income):** $580

- Box 3 (Ordinary Dividends): $200
- Box 4 (Net Long-Term Capital Gain): $1,200
- Box 12 (Charitable Contributions): $450

Step 4: Reporting on Individual Tax Return

1. **Mark Hunt's Form 1040:**
   - Line 8 (Ordinary Business Income): $101,040 (from Schedule K-1)
   - Line 2b (Interest Income): $580
   - Line 3b (Ordinary Dividends): $200
   - Line 13 (Capital Gains): $1,200
   - Schedule A (Charitable Contributions): $450

2. **Example Calculation:**
   - **Total Income:** $101,040 + $580 + $200 + $1,200 = $103,020
   - **Adjusted Gross Income (AGI):** $103,020
   - **Deductions (including charitable contributions):** Calculated on Schedule A.

Important Considerations

1. **Basis Calculation:**
   - **Initial Basis:** Mark's initial investment in Healthy Cupcakes Inc.
   - **Adjustments:** Include income, distributions, and contributions.
   - **Example:** If Mark's initial basis was $10,000 and he received $20,000 in distributions, his adjusted basis would be calculated as follows:
     - Initial Basis: $10,000
     -
       - Ordinary Income: $101,040
     -
       - Distributions: $20,000

- **Ending Basis:** $10,000 + $101,040 - $20,000 = $91,040

2. **Built-In Gains:**
    - **Definition:** Appreciated property that was part of the C Corporation before electing S status.
    - **Example:** If Healthy Cupcakes Inc. sold property within 10 years of becoming an S Corp, the built-in gain is calculated as the fair market value minus the adjusted basis at the date of conversion.

Conclusion:

Understanding and accurately filing S-Corporation taxes is crucial for compliance and effective financial management. By following the steps outlined in this chapter and using the example of Healthy Cupcakes Inc., you can confidently navigate the process of S-Corporation filing.

C-CORPORATION TAX RETURNS: A DETAILED GUIDE TO FORM 1120S (PART 1)

Introduction:

Filing taxes for a C-Corporation can be complex, but understanding the process step-by-step can make it more manageable. This chapter will provide a detailed walk-through of filing a C-Corporation tax return using Form 1120, with real-world examples to illustrate each step. Our example will focus on "Amusement Parks Inc." to help you understand the process.

Understanding C-Corporations

A C-Corporation (C Corp) is a legal entity that is separate from its owners, providing limited liability protection. It is subject to corporate income tax, and any distributions to shareholders are taxed again at the individual level, resulting in double taxation.

Key Characteristics of C-Corporations:

- **Limited Liability:** Shareholders are not personally liable for the debts of the corporation.
- **Unlimited Ownership:** There is no limit to the number of shareholders.
- **Taxation:** The corporation is taxed on its income, and shareholders are taxed on dividends.
- **Formation:** Created by filing Articles of Incorporation with the state.
- **Perpetual Existence:** Continues to exist even if ownership changes.

Filing Requirements

C-Corporations must file Form 1120 annually to report their income, gains, losses, deductions, credits, etc. Additionally, they must pay estimated taxes quarterly.

Real-World Example: Amusement Parks Inc.

Step 1: Basic Information and Income

1. **Form 1120 - Page 1:**
    - **Name and Address:** Enter "Amusement Parks Inc.", followed by the business address.
    - **EIN:** Enter the Employer Identification Number (EIN) of Amusement Parks Inc.

- Date Incorporated: January 1, 2010.
- Total Income:
    - Line 1a (Gross Receipts or Sales): $453,000
    - Line 5 (Interest Income): $3,564
    - Total Income: $453,000 + $3,564 = $456,564

Step 2: Deductions and Taxable Income

1. Deductions:
    - Line 12 (Compensation of Officers): $67,300
    - Line 13 (Salaries and Wages): $48,182
    - Line 14 (Repairs and Maintenance): $5,000
    - Line 16 (Bad Debts): $2,000
    - Line 17 (Rents): $14,200
    - Line 18 (Taxes and Licenses): $18,995
    - Line 19 (Interest): $4,000
    - Line 20 (Charitable Contributions): $1,000 (limited to 10% of taxable income)
    - Line 21 (Depreciation): $130,533
    - Line 22 (Advertising): $10,000
    - Line 26 (Other Deductions): $34,380
    - Total Deductions: $335,590
2. Taxable Income:
    - **Ordinary Business Income (Line 28):** $456,564 - $335,590 = $120,974
    - Taxable Income (Line 30): $120,974

Step 3: Calculating Tax Liability

1. Tax Calculation:

- **Tax Bracket:** For income between $0 and $50,000, the tax rate is 15%.
- **Tax Calculation for $50,000:** $50,000 * 15% = $7,500
- **Remaining Income:** $120,974 - $50,000 = $70,974
- **Tax Bracket for Remaining Income:** For income between $50,000 and $75,000, the tax rate is 25%.
- **Tax Calculation for $70,974:** $70,974 * 25% = $17,743.50
- **Total Tax Liability:** $7,500 + $17,743.50 = $25,243.50

Step 4: Reporting Estimated Tax Payments and Penalties

1. **Estimated Tax Payments:**
    - **Total Payments and Credits (Line 32):** Amusement Parks Inc. paid $12,000 in estimated taxes over the year.
    - **Tax Liability:** $25,243.50
    - **Total Payments:** $12,000

2. **Penalty for Underpayment:**
    - **Penalty (Line 33):** If there is a penalty for underpayment, it is reported here.
    - **Penalty Amount:** $160

3. **Amount Owed or Overpaid:**
    - **Overpayment (Line 34):** If total payments exceed the tax liability, the difference is an overpayment.
    - **Overpayment Amount:** $12,000 - $25,243.50 + $160 (penalty) = -$13,083.50 (amount owed)

Example: Understanding Double Taxation

1. **Corporate Taxation:**
    - **Taxable Income:** $120,974
    - **Corporate Tax:** $25,243.50

2. **Distribution to Shareholder:**

- **Distribution Amount:** $45,000 to shareholder Mike Smith
- **Individual Taxation:**
    - **Ordinary Dividends (Form 1040, Line 3a):** $45,000
    - **Tax Rate on Dividends:** Based on Mike's individual tax bracket

Conclusion:

Understanding and accurately filing C-Corporation taxes is crucial for compliance and effective financial management. By following the steps outlined in this chapter and using the example of Amusement Parks Inc., you can confidently navigate the process of C-Corporation filing.

ADVANCED C-CORPORATION FILING: NAVIGATING SPECIAL TAX SITUATIONS (PART 2)

Introduction:

In Part 1 of this chapter, we covered the basic income and deductions for C-Corporation tax filing. In this part, we will delve into some special transactions, adjustments, and deductions that C-Corporations may encounter. This detailed guide will help you understand these complexities with real-world examples, making the process more approachable for beginners.

Special C-Corporation Transactions

1. Property Transfers for Stock

When property is transferred to a corporation in exchange for stock, no gain or loss is recognized if the transferors control more than 80% of the corporation immediately after the exchange.

Example: Property Transfer for Stock

Dan, Mike, and Anna form a corporation, "Tech Innovations Inc." Dan transfers land, Mike transfers equipment, and Anna transfers cash, each receiving stock in return. They control 85% of the corporation after the transfer, so no gain or loss is recognized.

- **Dan's Contribution:**
    - Land valued at $50,000 for 25% of stock
- **Mike's Contribution:**
    - Equipment valued at $70,000 for 35% of stock
- **Anna's Contribution:**
    - Cash of $50,000 for 25% of stock

Since their combined ownership exceeds 80%, the transaction is not taxable.

2. Dividend Received Deduction (DRD)

The DRD allows a corporation to deduct a portion of the dividends received from other domestic corporations. The percentage of the deduction depends on the ownership percentage.

Example: Calculating DRD

"Tech Innovations Inc." received the following dividends:

- **$4,085 from a less than 20% owned domestic corporation**
    - DRD = $4,085 * 70% = $2,860
- **$3,500 from a 20%-80% owned domestic corporation**
    - DRD = $3,500 * 80% = $2,800
- **$5,000 from a wholly-owned subsidiary**
    - DRD = $5,000 * 100% = $5,000

Total DRD = $2,860 + $2,800 + $5,000 = $10,660

This deduction is reported on Line 29b of Form 1120.

3. Charitable Contributions

C-Corporations can deduct charitable contributions up to 10% of their adjusted taxable income, with any excess carried forward for five years.

Example: Charitable Contribution Deduction

"Tech Innovations Inc." made a charitable contribution of $5,000. The adjusted taxable income before the contribution and DRD is $48,890.

- **10% Limitation:** $48,890 * 10% = $4,889
- **Deductible Contribution:** $4,889 (excess $111 carried forward)

Report this deduction on Line 19 of Form 1120.

4. Accumulated Earnings Tax

Corporations may be subject to an accumulated earnings tax if they accumulate earnings beyond the reasonable needs of the business. This tax is designed to prevent corporations from avoiding shareholder taxation by retaining earnings.

Example: Assessing Accumulated Earnings Tax

"Tech Innovations Inc." retained $57,095 in earnings. As a manufacturing company, it can retain up to $250,000 without incurring this tax.

Since $57,095 is within this limit, no accumulated earnings tax is due.

5. Personal Holding Company Tax

A corporation is subject to personal holding company tax if more than 60% of its income is from passive sources and more than 50% of its stock is owned by five or fewer individuals.

Example: Personal Holding Company Tax

If "Tech Innovations Inc." earned 70% of its income from dividends and interest and is owned by three shareholders, it might be subject to this tax unless it pays out sufficient dividends to its shareholders.

6. Alternative Minimum Tax (AMT)

The AMT ensures that corporations with significant income pay at least a minimum amount of tax. It involves adjustments and preferences added to the regular taxable income to determine the alternative minimum taxable income (AMTI).

Example: Calculating AMT

"Tech Innovations Inc." has a regular taxable income of $48,886. Adjustments include $10,000 from private activity bond interest, resulting in an AMTI of $58,886. The AMT exemption is $40,000, reducing the AMTI to $18,886.

- **AMT Calculation:**
    - AMTI: $18,886
    - Exemption: $40,000
    - Taxable AMTI: $18,886 - $40,000 = $0 (no AMT due)

Conclusion:

Understanding these special transactions and deductions is crucial for accurately managing and filing C-Corporation taxes. By following the examples provided in this chapter, you can navigate these complexities with confidence and ensure compliance with tax regulations.

SECTION 2: TAXATION LAW

UNDERSTANDING COMMON LAW IN BUSINESS TAXATION

Introduction:

Common law forms the foundation of many legal systems and is crucial for understanding various aspects of business taxation. This chapter will guide you through the basics of common law, how it applies to business taxation, and provide clear examples to help you grasp the concepts. Using simple language, this guide aims to make common law accessible to beginners, aiding their learning and research.

What is Common Law?

Common law, also known as case law or precedent, is law that is developed through judicial decisions, as opposed to statutes or regulations enacted by legislative bodies. It evolves over time as judges make rulings in individual cases, setting precedents that future courts follow.

Key Features of Common Law:

1. **Precedent:** Judicial decisions serve as precedents for future cases, ensuring consistency and predictability in the legal system.
2. **Stare Decisis:** The principle that courts should follow precedents set by higher courts in the same jurisdiction.
3. **Judicial Interpretation:** Judges interpret and apply laws to specific cases, shaping the law through their rulings.

Common Law vs. Statutory Law

While statutory law is created by legislatures and written in legal codes, common law is developed through court decisions. Both play essential roles in the legal system, often working together to provide a comprehensive legal framework.

Example: Common Law in Business Taxation

Imagine a business dispute where the tax implications of a contract are in question. The court's decision in this case could set a precedent for how similar contracts are treated in future tax cases.

Common Law Contracts

Common law contracts are agreements governed by principles developed through court decisions. They typically involve services, real estate, and intangible assets. Common law requires specific elements for a contract to be valid:

1. **Offer:** One party must present a clear and definite proposal.
2. **Acceptance:** The other party must accept the offer without modifications.
3. **Consideration:** Both parties must exchange something of value.
4. **Mutual Assent:** Both parties must agree to the terms.
5. **Legality:** The contract's purpose must be lawful.

Example: Common Law Contract

Let's consider a scenario where Alice hires Bob to provide IT services for her company. Their agreement would be governed by common law because it involves a service contract. For the contract to be valid, Alice must offer to pay Bob a specific amount for his services, Bob must accept this offer, and both parties must exchange something of value (Alice's payment for Bob's services).

Common Law and Business Entities

Different business entities, such as partnerships and corporations, are subject to common law principles, especially regarding their formation, operation, and dissolution.

Example: Partnership Formation

Bob and John decide to form a partnership, "B&J Consulting." Under common law, their agreement must include:

- **Intent to Form a Partnership:** Both parties must intend to create a partnership.
- **Sharing of Profits and Losses:** The agreement must specify how profits and losses will be shared.
- **Joint Ownership and Management:** Both partners must have joint ownership and management responsibilities.

Common Law and Taxation

Common law significantly influences business taxation, particularly in areas not explicitly covered by statutory law. Courts interpret tax laws and regulations, setting precedents that impact future tax cases.

Example: Tax Treatment of a Common Law Contract

Consider a common law contract where a company agrees to provide consulting services for a fixed fee. The tax treatment of this contract may be influenced by court decisions on similar contracts, particularly regarding when income is recognized and what expenses are deductible.

Common Law Principles in Business Taxation

1. **Substance Over Form:** Courts often look at the substance of a transaction rather than its form to determine its tax treatment. This principle ensures that the economic reality of a transaction is considered over its legal structure.

2. **Economic Benefit Doctrine:** This doctrine states that if a taxpayer receives an economic benefit from a transaction, it may be taxable, even if it is not received in cash.

3. **Assignment of Income Doctrine:** This principle holds that income is taxed to the person who earns it, even if it is assigned to another person.

Example: Substance Over Form

A business structures a transaction to appear as a loan to avoid immediate taxation. However, if the substance of the transaction is actually a sale, the court may rule that it should be taxed as a sale, not a loan.

Conclusion:

Understanding common law principles is essential for navigating the complexities of business taxation. By learning how judicial decisions shape the law and influence tax treatment, you can better manage your business's legal and tax responsibilities.

UNDERSTANDING THE UNIFORM COMMERCIAL CODE (UCC) AND ITS APPLICATIONS IN BUSINESS TAXATION

Introduction:

The Uniform Commercial Code (UCC) plays a vital role in business transactions, particularly those involving goods. This chapter will guide you through the basics of the UCC, its applications, and key differences from common law. Using simple language and clear examples, this guide aims to make the UCC accessible to beginners, helping them understand and apply its principles in their business activities.

What is the Uniform Commercial Code (UCC)?

The UCC is a set of laws that govern commercial transactions in the United States. It is designed to provide a uniform and comprehensive set of rules to facilitate the sale and leasing of goods, negotiable instruments, and secured transactions.

Key Features of the UCC:

1. **Uniformity:** The UCC standardizes laws across different states to ensure consistency in commercial transactions.
2. **Flexibility:** The UCC allows for flexibility in contract terms, accommodating the needs of modern commerce.
3. **Focus on Goods:** The UCC primarily deals with transactions involving goods, which are defined as all things that are movable.

Differences Between UCC and Common Law

While common law governs contracts for services and real estate, the UCC specifically addresses contracts for the sale of goods. Here are some key differences:

1. **Definiteness of Terms:**
    - **Common Law:** Requires definite terms for a contract to be valid.
    - **UCC:** Allows for more flexibility; terms can be vague as long as there is an intent to contract and a reasonable basis for determining a remedy.

Example: Flexibility in UCC Contracts

Under the UCC, a wine merchant can offer to sell "as much wine as I can produce in one year" without specifying an exact quantity. This flexibility contrasts with common law, which would require more definite terms.

Essential Elements of a UCC Contract

Like common law, a UCC contract requires an offer, acceptance, and consideration. However, there are some differences in how these elements are treated under the UCC.

1. **Offer:**
   - An offer under the UCC can be vague and does not need to specify all terms. For instance, the price can be determined at a later date based on market rates.

Example: Offer in UCC Contract

A merchant offers to sell you a case of wine, with the price to be determined by the market rate at the time of delivery. This constitutes a valid offer under the UCC.

2. **Acceptance:**
   - Acceptance can include minor modifications to the offer. Unlike common law, the UCC does not require the "mirror image" of the offer for acceptance.

Example: Acceptance with Minor Changes

If a merchant offers to sell wine for cash, and you send a check instead, the UCC considers this an acceptance, as the change is minor. In common law, this would be a counteroffer.

3. **Consideration:**
   - Both parties must exchange something of value, but under the UCC, modifications to the contract do not require additional consideration.

Example: Consideration and Modification

A wine merchant agrees to sell wine at an increased price due to market changes. Under the UCC, this modification does not require new consideration from the buyer.

Title and Risk of Loss

The UCC specifies when the title and risk of loss transfer from the seller to the buyer, which can be crucial in determining liability for damaged goods.

1. **FOB Shipping Point:** Title and risk transfer when goods are shipped.
2. **FOB Destination:** Title and risk transfer when goods are delivered.

Example: Title and Risk Transfer

If a wine merchant ships wine FOB shipping point, the buyer assumes the risk once the wine leaves the warehouse. If the shipment is FOB destination, the risk remains with the seller until delivery.

Warranties Under the UCC

The UCC provides for several types of warranties to protect buyers, including:

1. **Warranty of Title:** Ensures the seller has the right to sell the goods and that they are free from liens.
2. **Warranty of Merchantability:** Goods must be fit for their ordinary purpose.
3. **Warranty of Fitness for a Particular Purpose:** Applies when a seller knows the buyer relies on their expertise to select suitable goods.

Example: Warranty of Merchantability

A buyer purchases a lawnmower from a merchant. The warranty of merchantability guarantees that the lawnmower will function as a lawnmower should. If it does not, the buyer may have a claim under this warranty.

Remedies for Breach of Contract

The UCC provides remedies for both buyers and sellers in the event of a breach of contract.

1. **Seller's Remedies:** Include canceling the contract, withholding delivery, and seeking damages.
2. **Buyer's Remedies:** Include rejecting nonconforming goods, seeking specific performance, and claiming damages.

Example: Remedies for Breach

If a wine merchant delivers spoiled wine, the buyer can reject the goods and demand a refund or replacement. If the buyer breaches the contract by refusing to accept conforming goods, the seller can seek damages for the lost sale.

Conclusion:

Understanding the UCC is essential for navigating commercial transactions involving goods. By familiarizing yourself with its principles and differences from common law, you can ensure your business operations comply with legal standards and effectively manage your contractual obligations.

UNDERSTANDING AGENCY LAW IN BUSINESS: KEY CONCEPTS AND APPLICATIONS

Introduction:

Agency law is a fundamental concept in business operations, governing the relationships where one party, the agent, acts on behalf of another party, the principal. This chapter will provide a comprehensive guide to understanding agency law, its key elements, and how it applies in business contexts. Using simple language and clear examples, this guide aims to make agency law accessible to beginners, helping them navigate their business responsibilities effectively.

What is Agency Law?

Agency law involves a three-party relationship where the principal authorizes the agent to act on their behalf in dealings with third parties. The agent's actions bind the principal in contracts and other transactions with the third parties.

Key Parties in Agency Law:

1. **Principal:** The person who authorizes the agent to act on their behalf.
2. **Agent:** The person authorized to act on behalf of the principal.
3. **Third Party:** The person or entity with whom the agent interacts on behalf of the principal.

Example: Agency Relationship

Alice (Principal) hires Bob (Agent) to negotiate a contract with Charlie (Third Party) on her behalf. If Bob successfully negotiates the contract, Alice and Charlie are bound by its terms.

Types of Principals

1. **Fully Disclosed Principal:**
   - The third party knows the identity of the principal.
   - **Example:** Bob informs Charlie that he is negotiating on behalf of Alice.
2. **Partially Disclosed Principal:**
   - The third party knows an agent is acting on behalf of a principal but does not know the principal's identity.

- **Example:** Bob tells Charlie he is representing someone but does not disclose Alice's name.

3. **Undisclosed Principal:**
    - The third party believes the agent is acting on their own behalf.
    - **Example:** Bob negotiates with Charlie without mentioning he is representing Alice.

Authority of Agents

Agents can bind principals to contracts through various types of authority:

1. **Actual Authority:**
    - **Express Authority:** Explicitly granted by the principal.
        - **Example:** Alice explicitly tells Bob to buy 1,000 units of a product.
    - **Implied Authority:** Authority inferred from the agent's duties.
        - **Example:** Bob, as a purchasing manager, is expected to order supplies as needed.

2. **Apparent Authority:**
    - Based on the third party's perception that the agent has authority.
        - **Example:** If Bob has previously purchased products on behalf of Alice, Charlie might reasonably believe Bob has the authority to do so again.

Fiduciary Duties of Agents

Agents owe fiduciary duties to their principals, including:

1. **Duty of Loyalty:** Acting in the best interests of the principal.
2. **Duty of Care:** Acting with the care that a reasonably prudent person would use.
3. **Duty of Obedience:** Following the principal's instructions.

Example: Fiduciary Duty

If Bob, as Alice's agent, learns of a business opportunity, he must inform Alice and cannot take the opportunity for himself.

Types of Agents

1. **General Agent:** Has broad authority to act on behalf of the principal in a variety of matters.
    - **Example:** A business manager who handles all business operations.
2. **Special Agent:** Has limited authority to act in a specific transaction.
    - **Example:** A real estate agent authorized to sell a particular property.
3. **Sub-Agent:** Appointed by another agent with the principal's consent.
    - **Example:** Bob appoints Clara as a sub-agent to assist in purchasing goods for Alice.

Agency Coupled with an Interest

An agency coupled with an interest occurs when the agent has a vested interest in the subject matter of the agency.

Example: Agency Coupled with Interest

Alice borrows money from a bank to purchase a property, and the bank acts as her agent in dealing with the mortgage company. The bank has an interest in the property and cannot be dismissed by Alice without settling the debt.

Liability in Agency Relationships

1. **Principal's Liability:**
    - The principal is liable for contracts entered into by the agent within their authority.
    - **Example:** If Bob orders goods within his authority, Alice must pay for them.
2. **Agent's Liability:**
    - The agent may be liable if they act outside their authority or if the principal is undisclosed.
    - **Example:** If Bob exceeds his authority and orders more goods than allowed, he may be personally liable.

Termination of Agency

An agency relationship can be terminated by:

1. **Mutual Agreement:** Both parties agree to end the relationship.
2. **Unilateral Termination:** Either party can terminate, though there may be consequences for breach of contract.
3. **Operation of Law:** The agency ends automatically due to events like the death of the principal or agent, bankruptcy, or the subject matter becoming illegal.

Example: Termination by Operation of Law

If Alice, the principal, dies, the agency relationship with Bob automatically ends, and Bob can no longer act on her behalf.

Conclusion:

Understanding agency law is essential for managing business relationships and ensuring that actions taken on your behalf are legally binding and in your best interests. By following the principles outlined in this chapter and considering the examples provided, you can effectively navigate the complexities of agency law in your business operations.

UNDERSTANDING BANKRUPTCY LAW IN BUSINESS TAXATION

Introduction:

Bankruptcy law can be complex, but understanding its basics is crucial for managing financial distress in a business. This chapter will guide you through the different types of bankruptcy, their rules, and how they apply to various business entities. Using simple language and clear examples, this guide aims to make bankruptcy law accessible to beginners, helping them navigate through financial challenges effectively.

What is Bankruptcy?

Bankruptcy is a legal process for individuals or businesses that are unable to repay their outstanding debts. It provides a fresh start by discharging debts or structuring a plan to repay them. Bankruptcy can be voluntary, initiated by the debtor, or involuntary, initiated by creditors.

Types of Bankruptcy Filings

1. **Chapter 7: Liquidation**
    - **Description:** This type involves the complete liquidation of a debtor's non-exempt assets to pay creditors.
    - **Eligibility:** Both individuals and businesses can file for Chapter 7.
    - **Process:** A trustee is appointed to oversee the liquidation of assets and distribution of proceeds to creditors.
    - **Outcome:** Remaining debts are discharged, giving the debtor a fresh start.

Example: Chapter 7 Bankruptcy

ABC Manufacturing, a small business, cannot pay its debts. The company files for Chapter 7, and a trustee is appointed. The trustee sells the company's equipment, inventory, and other assets. The proceeds are distributed to creditors. Remaining debts are discharged, and the business ceases operations.

2. **Chapter 11: Reorganization**
    - **Description:** This type allows businesses to continue operating while restructuring their debts.

- **Eligibility:** Mostly businesses, but individuals with substantial debts can also file.
- **Process:** The debtor proposes a reorganization plan to keep the business running and pay creditors over time. Creditors vote on the plan.
- **Outcome:** Debts are reorganized, and the business continues operations under a court-approved plan.

Example: Chapter 11 Bankruptcy

XYZ Corp, a large retailer, faces financial trouble. It files for Chapter 11 and proposes a reorganization plan. The plan includes closing unprofitable stores and negotiating new terms with suppliers. Creditors approve the plan, allowing XYZ Corp to continue operating and eventually emerge from bankruptcy.

3. **Chapter 13: Repayment Plan**
   - **Description:** This type allows individuals with regular income to develop a plan to repay all or part of their debts.
   - **Eligibility:** Only individuals (not businesses) with regular income.
   - **Process:** The debtor proposes a repayment plan, typically lasting three to five years, to pay creditors.
   - **Outcome:** Debts are repaid according to the plan, and any remaining dischargeable debts are wiped out.

Example: Chapter 13 Bankruptcy

Jane, a freelance graphic designer, is struggling with debt. She files for Chapter 13, proposing a five-year repayment plan. Her plan is approved by the court, allowing her to pay back her creditors in manageable installments while keeping her assets.

Key Concepts in Bankruptcy Law

1. **Automatic Stay:**
   - Upon filing for bankruptcy, an automatic stay is issued, halting most collection activities, lawsuits, and foreclosures.
   - **Example:** When XYZ Corp files for Chapter 11, an automatic stay prevents creditors from pursuing collection actions.
2. **Trustee:**

- In Chapter 7 and Chapter 13 cases, a trustee is appointed to manage the bankruptcy process, including asset liquidation and distribution of funds.
- **Example:** In ABC Manufacturing's Chapter 7 case, the trustee sells the company's assets and distributes the proceeds to creditors.

3. **Discharge:**
   - A discharge releases the debtor from personal liability for certain types of debts, preventing creditors from taking any action to collect those debts.
   - **Example:** After completing her Chapter 13 repayment plan, Jane receives a discharge of her remaining unsecured debts.

Voluntary vs. Involuntary Bankruptcy

1. **Voluntary Bankruptcy:**
   - The debtor initiates the filing.
   - **Example:** ABC Manufacturing files for Chapter 7 to liquidate its assets and discharge debts.

2. **Involuntary Bankruptcy:**
   - Creditors initiate the filing against a debtor who is not paying debts.
   - **Example:** Creditors file an involuntary Chapter 7 petition against a non-paying company, proving insolvency.

Special Considerations in Bankruptcy

1. **Exempt and Non-Exempt Assets:**
   - Exempt assets are those the debtor can keep, while non-exempt assets are sold to pay creditors.
   - **Example:** In Jane's Chapter 13 case, her primary residence and personal vehicle are exempt assets.

2. **Priority of Claims:**
   - Claims are paid in a specific order: secured creditors, administrative expenses, wages, taxes, and unsecured creditors.

- **Example:** In ABC Manufacturing's Chapter 7 case, secured creditors are paid first from the proceeds of asset sales.

3. **Fraudulent Transfers and Preferences:**
    - Transfers made to defraud creditors or preferential payments to certain creditors before filing can be voided by the trustee.
    - **Example:** If Jane transferred assets to a friend before filing, the trustee could void the transfer and reclaim the assets.

Conclusion:

Understanding bankruptcy law is crucial for managing financial difficulties in business. By familiarizing yourself with the types of bankruptcy, key concepts, and special considerations, you can navigate the process more effectively and make informed decisions.

SECTION 3: SPECIAL TAX SITUATIONS

DEPRECIATION DEMYSTIFIED: BASICS AND TAX CALCULATION METHODS

Introduction:

Depreciation is a standard tax concept, but special situations can complicate its application. This chapter will delve into these special tax situations, including changes in business use, partial asset dispositions, and bonus depreciation. We will use clear examples to illustrate each scenario, making it accessible to beginners.

Special Tax Situations Involving Depreciation

1. **Changes in Business Use**
2. **Partial Asset Dispositions**
3. **Bonus Depreciation**
4. **Listed Property**

1. Changes in Business Use

When an asset's use changes from business to personal, or vice versa, the treatment of depreciation changes accordingly.

Example: Change from Business to Personal Use

John buys a computer for his business for $2,000 and uses it exclusively for business in Year 1. In Year 2, he starts using it 50% for personal use.

Year 1 Depreciation:

- **Depreciation Method:** MACRS
- **Recovery Period:** 5 years
- **Convention:** Half-year
- **Depreciation:** $2,000 * 20% = $400

Year 2 Depreciation:

- **Adjusted Basis:** $2,000 - $400 = $1,600
- **Depreciation:** $1,600 * 32% * 50% = $256

John must adjust his depreciation calculations to reflect the personal use.

2. Partial Asset Dispositions

When part of an asset is disposed of or retired, special rules apply for calculating depreciation.

Example: Partial Disposition of a Building

XYZ Corp owns a building valued at $500,000 and replaces the roof, valued at $50,000.

Initial Depreciation:

- **Depreciation Method:** MACRS
- **Recovery Period:** 39 years
- **Convention:** Mid-month
- **Annual Depreciation:** $500,000 / 39 = $12,820.51

Disposition and New Roof:

- **Adjust Basis:** Reduce building basis by roof value ($500,000 - $50,000 = $450,000)
- **Depreciation for New Roof:** $50,000 / 39 = $1,282.05 annually

XYZ Corp must adjust depreciation schedules to reflect the new roof and retired old roof.

3. Bonus Depreciation

Bonus depreciation allows businesses to take an additional deduction in the year an asset is placed in service.

Example: Using Bonus Depreciation

ABC Manufacturing purchases equipment for $100,000 in 2021.

Bonus Depreciation (100%):

- **Year 1 Deduction:** $100,000 * 100% = $100,000

Regular Depreciation:

- No additional regular depreciation is needed for this asset in subsequent years.

ABC Manufacturing can fully deduct the equipment cost in the first year.

4. Listed Property

Listed property includes items like vehicles and computers, which require special rules if used for both business and personal purposes.

Example: Depreciation for a Business Vehicle

Linda purchases a car for $30,000 and uses it 60% for business.

Year 1 Depreciation:

- **Depreciation Method:** MACRS
- **Recovery Period:** 5 years
- **Business Use Percentage:** 60%
- **Depreciation:** $30,000 * 20% * 60% = $3,600

Linda must maintain records to substantiate the business use percentage.

Form 4562: Reporting Special Depreciation

Form 4562 is used to report depreciation and amortization. Special situations are reported in specific sections.

Example: Reporting on Form 4562

Let's consolidate our examples:

1. **Section 179 Deduction:** Report $50,000 for new equipment.
2. **MACRS Depreciation:**
    - John's Computer: $400 Year 1, $256 Year 2 (adjusted for personal use)
    - XYZ Corp's Building: $12,820.51 annually (adjusted for partial disposition)
3. **Bonus Depreciation:** $100,000 for ABC Manufacturing's equipment.
4. **Listed Property:** $3,600 for Linda's vehicle.

Section I: Election to Expense Certain Property Under Section 179

- **Line 6:** Report $50,000 for equipment.

Section II: Special Depreciation Allowance and Other Depreciation

- **Line 14:** Report $100,000 for bonus depreciation.

Section V: Listed Property

- **Line 26:** Report $3,600 for Linda's vehicle.

Conclusion:

Understanding special depreciation situations is essential for accurate tax reporting. By familiarizing yourself with the rules and calculations for changes in business use, partial dispositions, bonus depreciation, and listed property, you can ensure compliance and optimize tax benefits.

SECTION 179 EXPLAINED: HOW TO MAXIMIZE ITS TAX BENEFITS FOR YOUR BUSINESS

Introduction:

Section 179 is a powerful tax deduction that allows businesses to immediately expense the cost of qualifying property, rather than capitalizing and depreciating it over time. This chapter will guide you through the basics of Section 179, its limitations, and how to maximize its benefits in various scenarios. Using simple language and clear examples, this guide aims to make Section 179 accessible to beginners, helping them optimize their tax savings.

What is Section 179?

Section 179 of the Internal Revenue Code allows businesses to deduct the full purchase price of qualifying equipment and/or software purchased or financed during the tax year. This incentive was created to encourage businesses to invest in themselves by purchasing needed equipment and technology.

Key Features of Section 179:

1. **Immediate Deduction:** Allows businesses to deduct the full cost of qualifying property in the year it is placed in service.

2. **Deduction Limit:** The maximum deduction limit varies by year. For instance, in 2017, the limit was $500,000.

3. **Investment Limit:** The total amount of equipment purchased cannot exceed a certain threshold, which was $2,000,000 in 2017.

Qualifying Property:

- **Tangible Personal Property:** Includes machinery, equipment, furniture, and vehicles.

- **Off-the-Shelf Software:** Software purchased off the shelf and used in business.

- **Certain Improvements to Nonresidential Property:** Such as roofs, HVAC, fire protection systems, alarm systems, and security systems.

Example: Utilizing Section 179 Deduction

ABC Manufacturing purchases a piece of equipment for $650,000 in 2017 and elects to use the Section 179 deduction.

1. **Initial Deduction Calculation:**
   - Total Cost of Equipment: $650,000
   - Section 179 Deduction Limit for 2017: $500,000
   - Bonus Depreciation (50% of remaining amount): $75,000 (50% of $150,000)
   - Regular Depreciation (remaining amount): $15,000 (20% of $75,000)
2. **Total First-Year Deduction:**
   - Section 179 Deduction: $500,000
   - Bonus Depreciation: $75,000
   - Regular Depreciation: $15,000
   - Total Deduction: $590,000

By electing Section 179, ABC Manufacturing can deduct $590,000 in the first year, significantly reducing its taxable income.

Limitations and Considerations:

1. **Business Income Limitation:** The total amount of the Section 179 deduction cannot exceed the total taxable income derived from the active conduct of a trade or business during the year.
2. **Carryover of Disallowed Deduction:** If the deduction exceeds the business income limitation, the excess amount can be carried forward to future years.
3. **Listed Property:** Certain property, such as vehicles, must meet specific requirements to qualify for the Section 179 deduction.

Example: Business Income Limitation

XYZ Corp has a taxable income of $450,000 before the Section 179 deduction and purchases $500,000 worth of equipment.

1. **Section 179 Deduction:** $450,000 (limited to taxable income)
2. **Carryover Amount:** $50,000 (excess deduction carried forward to next year)

XYZ Corp can only deduct $450,000 in the current year due to the business income limitation, with the remaining $50,000 carried forward.

Form 4562: Reporting Section 179 Deduction

Form 4562 is used to report depreciation and amortization, including the Section 179 deduction. It includes sections for reporting the cost of qualifying property, the amount of the deduction, and any carryover amounts.

Example: Completing Form 4562

Let's revisit the example of ABC Manufacturing:

1. **Part I - Election to Expense Certain Property Under Section 179:**
    - **Line 1:** Cost of Section 179 property: $650,000
    - **Line 2:** Dollar limitation: $500,000
    - **Line 5:** Elected cost: $500,000
2. **Part II - Special Depreciation Allowance and Other Depreciation:**
    - **Line 14:** Special depreciation allowance: $75,000
3. **Part III - MACRS Depreciation:**
    - **Line 17:** Depreciation deduction: $15,000

By accurately completing Form 4562, ABC Manufacturing ensures it claims the maximum allowable deduction.

Maximizing Section 179 Benefits

To fully utilize the Section 179 deduction, businesses should plan their equipment purchases and consider the timing of placing assets in service.

Example: Strategic Planning for Section 179

Jane's Bakery plans to purchase $800,000 worth of equipment over two years. By splitting the purchases—$400,000 each year—Jane can maximize the Section 179 deduction, avoiding the investment limit and spreading the tax benefit.

Conclusion:

Understanding and utilizing the Section 179 deduction is crucial for optimizing tax savings and encouraging business investment. By familiarizing yourself with the rules and limitations, you can effectively manage your business's tax responsibilities and maximize benefits.

PROPERTY TRANSACTIONS (1231): WHAT YOU NEED TO KNOW FOR TAX BENEFITS

Introduction:

Property transactions under Section 1231 can significantly impact your tax liability. Understanding how to classify and treat these transactions is crucial for maximizing tax benefits and ensuring compliance. This chapter will guide you through Section 1231 property transactions, including definitions, classifications, and tax implications. We will use clear examples to illustrate each concept, making it accessible to beginners.

What is Section 1231?

Section 1231 of the Internal Revenue Code pertains to the tax treatment of gains and losses from the sale or exchange of certain types of business property. These properties are generally depreciable or real property used in a trade or business and held for more than one year.

Key Concepts in Section 1231:

1. **1231 Property:** Includes depreciable and real property used in business, held for more than one year.

2. **Ordinary Income and Capital Gains:** Gains from 1231 property may be treated as long-term capital gains, while losses are treated as ordinary losses.

3. **Recapture Rules:** Specific rules apply to recapture depreciation taken on the property.

Types of 1231 Property:

1. **Depreciable Personal Property:** Equipment, machinery, and vehicles used in business.

2. **Real Property:** Buildings, factories, rental properties used in business.

Example: Classifying Section 1231 Property

ABC Manufacturing owns a piece of machinery used in production, purchased three years ago, and an office building used for business operations, held for more than a year. Both assets qualify as 1231 property.

Tax Treatment of Section 1231 Gains and Losses

1. **Net Gain:** Treated as long-term capital gain, which benefits from lower tax rates.
2. **Net Loss:** Treated as ordinary loss, which can offset ordinary income without limitation.

Example: 1231 Gain and Loss Calculation

Scenario 1: 1231 Gain

- **Machinery Cost:** $10,000
- **Depreciation Taken:** $4,000
- **Adjusted Basis:** $10,000 - $4,000 = $6,000
- **Sale Price:** $11,000
- **Total Gain:** $11,000 - $6,000 = $5,000

The $5,000 gain is a 1231 gain, treated as long-term capital gain.

Scenario 2: 1231 Loss

- **Building Cost:** $600,000
- **Depreciation Taken:** $540,000
- **Adjusted Basis:** $600,000 - $540,000 = $60,000
- **Sale Price:** $50,000
- **Total Loss:** $60,000 - $50,000 = $10,000

The $10,000 loss is a 1231 loss, treated as an ordinary loss.

Recapture Rules for Section 1231 Property

1. **Section 1245 Property (Personal Property):**
   - Recaptures all depreciation as ordinary income.
   - **Example:** Sold machinery with $4,000 depreciation taken, resulting in a $5,000 gain. The $4,000 is recaptured as ordinary income, and the remaining $1,000 is a 1231 gain.

2. **Section 1250 Property (Real Property):**

- Recaptures excess depreciation over straight-line depreciation as ordinary income.
- **Example:** Sold building with accelerated depreciation exceeding straight-line by $30,000, resulting in a $440,000 gain. The $30,000 is recaptured as ordinary income, and the remaining $410,000 is a 1231 gain.

Special Considerations:

1. **Look-Back Rule:**
   - Requires net 1231 gains to be reclassified as ordinary income to the extent of any nonrecaptured net 1231 losses from the past five years.
   - **Example:** If you had a net 1231 loss of $10,000 three years ago and a net 1231 gain of $15,000 this year, $10,000 of the gain will be reclassified as ordinary income.

Example: Applying the Look-Back Rule

- **Year 1:** $10,000 net 1231 loss
- **Year 3:** $15,000 net 1231 gain
- **Reclassified Gain:** $10,000 as ordinary income, $5,000 as long-term capital gain

Form 4797: Reporting Property Transactions

Form 4797 is used to report sales of business property. This form categorizes the transactions to determine the correct tax treatment.

Example: Completing Form 4797

Let's revisit the example of ABC Manufacturing:

1. **Part I - Sales or Exchanges of Property Used in a Trade or Business and Involuntary Conversions:**
   - **Line 2:** Describe the property (e.g., machinery), date acquired, date sold, gross sales price, cost or other basis, depreciation allowed, and gain or loss.
2. **Part III - Gain from Disposition of Property Under Sections 1245, 1250, 1252, 1254, and 1255:**

- **Line 19:** Gain from Section 1245 property (machinery).

By accurately completing Form 4797, ABC Manufacturing ensures proper reporting and tax treatment of its property transactions.

Conclusion:

Understanding and managing Section 1231 property transactions is essential for optimizing tax outcomes and ensuring compliance. By familiarizing yourself with the classification, tax treatment, and recapture rules, you can effectively manage your business's property transactions and maximize tax benefits.

SPECIAL PROPERTY TRANSACTIONS: A BUSINESS TAX GUIDE

Introduction:

Special property transactions can significantly impact your tax liability. Understanding the rules and nuances of these transactions is crucial for ensuring compliance and optimizing tax benefits. This chapter will cover special property transactions, including gifts, like-kind exchanges, involuntary conversions, home sales, wash sales, related-party transactions, and installment sales. We will use simple language and clear examples to make these concepts accessible to beginners.

1. Property Received as a Gift

When you receive a property as a gift, special rules apply to determine the basis for calculating gains or losses when you sell the property.

Rules for Gifted Property:

- **Gain Basis:** Use the donor's basis (the original cost to the giver).
- **Loss Basis:** Use the lesser of the donor's basis or the fair market value (FMV) at the time of the gift.
- **No Gain or Loss:** If sold between the donor's basis and the FMV, no gain or loss is recognized.

Example: Gifted Property Transactions

1. **Gain Scenario:**
    - Donor's Basis: $30,000
    - FMV at Gift Date: $10,000
    - Sale Price: $39,000
    - **Gain Calculation:** $39,000 - $30,000 = $9,000 gain
2. **Loss Scenario:**
    - Donor's Basis: $30,000
    - FMV at Gift Date: $10,000
    - Sale Price: $9,000
    - **Loss Calculation:** $9,000 - $10,000 = $1,000 loss

3. **No Gain or Loss Scenario:**
    - Donor's Basis: $30,000
    - FMV at Gift Date: $10,000
    - Sale Price: $20,000
    - **No Gain or Loss:** Sale price is between donor's basis and FMV.

2. Like-Kind Exchanges

A like-kind exchange allows you to defer paying taxes on the gain of a property if you reinvest the proceeds in similar property.

Requirements for Like-Kind Exchanges:

- Must exchange real property for real property or personal business property for similar personal business property.
- Recognize gain equal to the lesser of the realized gain or the boot received (cash or unlike property).

Example: Like-Kind Exchange

- Give up: Land worth $10,000
- Receive: Land worth $9,000 + Car worth $2,000 + Cash $1,500 (total $12,500)
- **Boot Calculation:** $1,500 (cash) + $2,000 (car) = $3,500
- **Realized Gain:** $12,500 (received) - $10,000 (given up) = $2,500
- **Recognized Gain:** Lesser of realized gain ($2,500) or boot received ($3,500) = $2,500

3. Involuntary Conversions

Involuntary conversions occur when property is destroyed, stolen, or condemned, and you receive money or other property as compensation.

Rules for Involuntary Conversions:

- No gain recognized if you reinvest all proceeds in similar property.
- Gain recognized is the lesser of the realized gain or the amount not reinvested.

Example: Involuntary Conversion

- Basis in Property: $20,000
- Proceeds Received: $24,000
- Realized Gain: $24,000 - $20,000 = $4,000
- Reinvested Amount: $21,000
- Amount Not Reinvested: $24,000 - $21,000 = $3,000
- **Recognized Gain:** Lesser of realized gain ($4,000) or amount not reinvested ($3,000) = $3,000
- **New Basis in Property:** $21,000 (reinvested) - $1,000 (deferred gain) = $20,000

4. Home Sales

Special rules apply when you sell your primary residence.

Rules for Home Sales:

- Exclude up to $250,000 ($500,000 for married filing jointly) of gain if you owned and lived in the home for at least two of the last five years.
- Losses on the sale of your home are not deductible.

Example: Home Sale Exclusion

- Sale Price: $400,000
- Basis in Home: $200,000
- Gain: $400,000 - $200,000 = $200,000
- **Exclusion:** $200,000 gain is fully excluded (below $250,000 threshold).

5. Wash Sales

A wash sale occurs when you sell a stock at a loss and repurchase the same or substantially identical stock within 30 days.

Rules for Wash Sales:

- Losses from wash sales are not deductible.
- The disallowed loss is added to the basis of the repurchased stock.

Example: Wash Sale

- Sell Stock: January 1 for $1,000 (basis $1,500, $500 loss)
- Repurchase Same Stock: January 15 for $1,200
- **Disallowed Loss:** $500
- **New Basis in Stock:** $1,200 (repurchase price) + $500 (disallowed loss) = $1,700

6. Related-Party Transactions

Special rules apply when you sell property to related parties.

Rules for Related-Party Transactions:

- Losses are not deductible.
- Gains are always recognized.

Example: Related-Party Sale

- Sell to Brother: Property for $5,000 (basis $6,000, $1,000 loss)
- **Loss:** Not deductible
- Sell to Brother: Property for $8,000 (basis $6,000, $2,000 gain)
- **Gain:** $2,000 recognized

7. Installment Sales

An installment sale is a sale where you receive at least one payment after the tax year of the sale.

Rules for Installment Sales:

- Recognize gain over the period you receive payments.
- Calculate gross profit percentage: (Gross Profit / Sales Price) * Payment Received = Gain Recognized.

Example: Installment Sale

- Sale Price: $1,000
- Basis: $800
- Gross Profit: $1,000 - $800 = $200
- Gross Profit Percentage: $200 / $1,000 = 20%

- Payment Received: $100
- **Recognized Gain:** $100 * 20% = $20

Conclusion:

Understanding special property transactions is crucial for accurate tax reporting and optimizing tax benefits. By familiarizing yourself with the rules and examples provided, you can navigate these complex situations and ensure compliance.

CONCLUSION

As we reach the conclusion of **"Mastering Business Taxes: The Ultimate Guide, Tips, Insights and Strategies for Small Business Owners, LLCs, S-Corps & Sole Proprietors to Maximizing Profits and Minimizing Liability,"** it's time to reflect on the journey we've embarked upon and the wealth of knowledge we've uncovered together. This book was designed to transform the often daunting subject of business taxation into a powerful tool for your business's success.

Harness the Power of Knowledge

The chapters you've explored provide a comprehensive framework to navigate the complex world of business taxes. From understanding the foundational principles in Section 1, exploring the intricacies of taxation law in Section 2, to mastering special tax situations in Section 3, you are now equipped with the insights and strategies needed to optimize your tax outcomes. The knowledge you've gained is not just theoretical; it's a practical roadmap to transforming your business operations and financial health.

Take Action and Implement Strategies

Now is the time to act. The true value of this guide lies in its application. Review your current tax strategies and identify areas where you can implement the tips and insights from this book. Whether it's choosing the right business structure, leveraging the pass-through tax break, or maximizing deductions through Section 179, each step you take can lead to significant financial benefits and business growth.

Engage with Professionals

While this book has provided you with a solid foundation, remember that the world of taxation is dynamic and complex. Engaging with tax professionals can further enhance your understanding and application of the principles covered. Don't hesitate to seek expert advice to tailor strategies specifically to your business's needs and to stay updated on the latest tax laws and regulations.

Stay Informed and Adaptive

Tax laws and regulations are continually evolving. Staying informed about these changes is crucial for maintaining an optimal tax strategy. Regularly consult trusted sources, participate in relevant workshops, and continue your education to ensure your business remains compliant and takes full advantage of available tax benefits.

Your Path to Business Success

Mastering business taxes is a continuous journey, but one that is well worth the effort. The strategies and insights from this book provide you with the tools to minimize liability, maximize profits, and ensure the long-term success of your business. Your commitment to understanding and applying these principles will set you apart and position your business for sustainable growth.

Final Thoughts

Thank you for choosing this guide as your companion in mastering business taxes. Your dedication to improving your tax strategies will undoubtedly yield significant rewards. As you move forward, remember that every informed decision you make is a step towards greater financial health and business excellence. Embrace the knowledge you've gained, act on the strategies provided, and watch your business thrive.

Here's to your continued success and mastery of business taxes.

CHECK OUT OTHER BOOKS

Go here to check out other related books that might interest you:

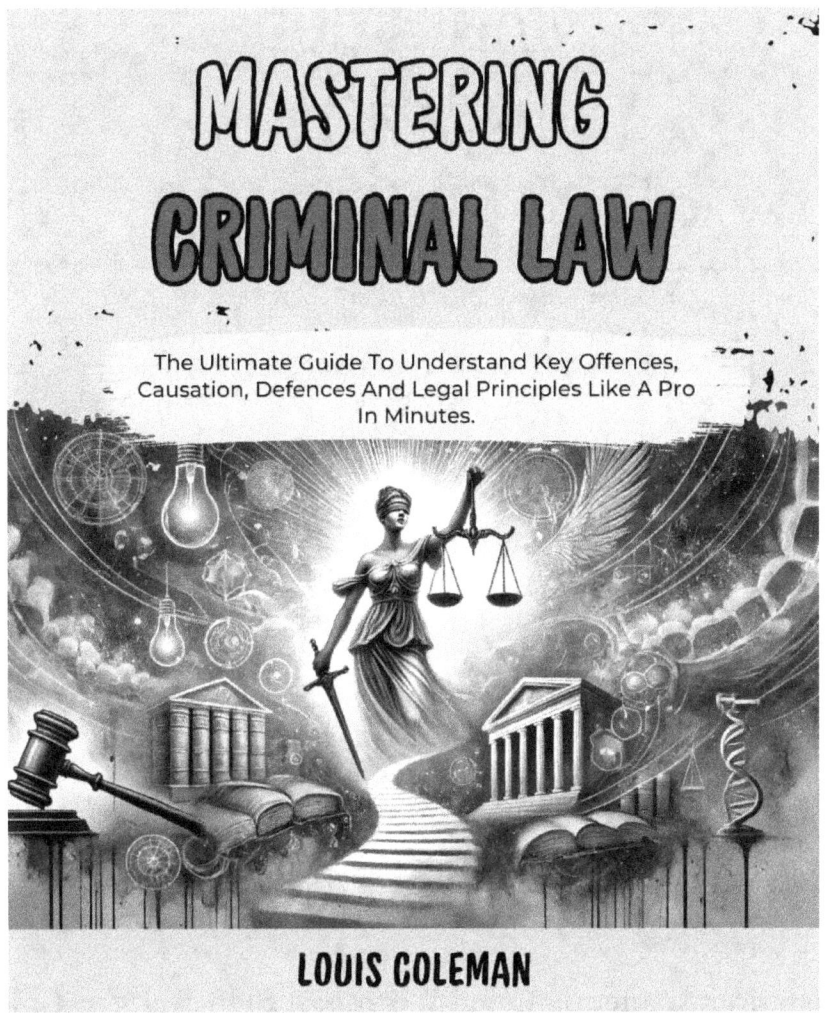

Mastering Criminal Law: The Ultimate Guide To Understand Key Offences, Causation, Defences And Legal Principles Like A Pro In Minutes.

https://www.amazon.com/dp/B0D4H97Y7B

Mastering Academic Legal Writing: A Step-By-Step Guide, Proven Techniques, Tips And Strategies For Crafting Powerful And Compelling Legal Documents Like A Pro In Minutes.

https://www.amazon.com/dp/B0D7J6FNTY

Mastering Business Writing: A Step-By-Step Guide, Proven Techniques, Tips & Strategies For Crafting Powerful And Compelling Business Letters, Reports, Proposals and Emails Like A Pro In Minutes.

https://www.amazon.com/dp/B0D7N1Y8VM

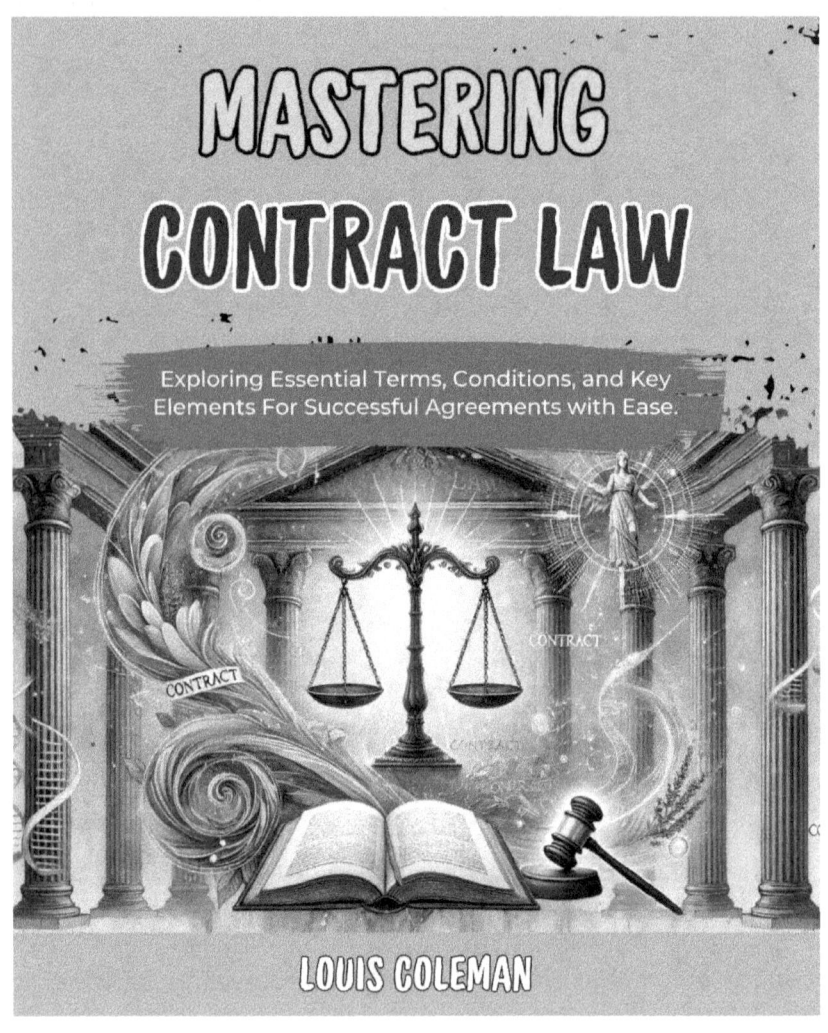

Mastering Contract Law: Exploring Essential Terms, Conditions, and Key Elements For Successful Agreements with Ease.

https://www.amazon.com/dp/B0D7Q6QRF5

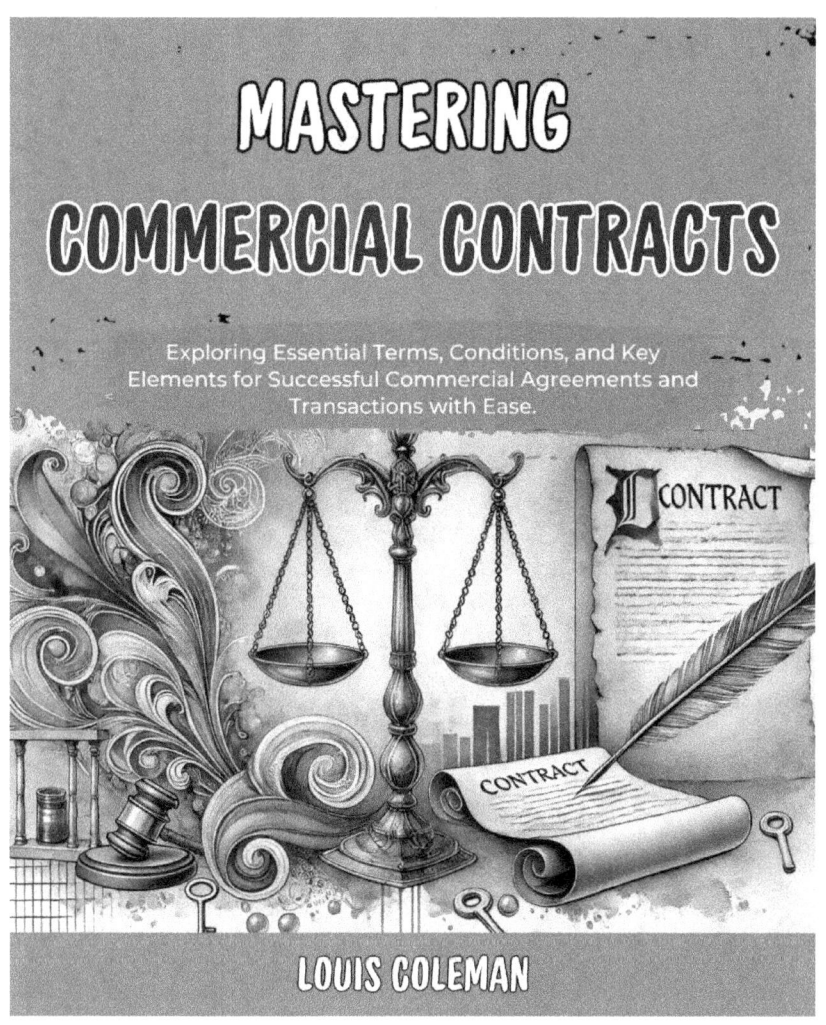

Mastering Commercial Contracts: Exploring Essential Terms, Conditions, and Key Elements For Successful Commercial Agreements and Transactions with Ease.

https://www.amazon.com/dp/B0D7TRSYLM

Mastering Commercial Law: Your Ultimate Guide to Understanding Key Business Structures and Terms Related To Sole Proprietorships, Partnerships, and Corporations Like A Pro In Minutes.

https://www.amazon.com/dp/B0D7W67S34

Mastering Legal Tech And AI: Tools, Trends, Innovations, and Transformations That Lawyers, Law Students and Professional Must Know in Modern Law Practice and Justice.

https://www.amazon.com/dp/B0D81KTZPN

Mastering Business Taxes: The Ultimate Guide, Tips, Insights and Strategies For Small Business Owners, LLCs, S-Corps & Sole Proprietors To Maximizing Profits And Minimizing Liability (Book 1).

https://www.amazon.com/dp/B0D844QWM5

Kindle Publishing Guidelines: The Ultimate Guide, Tips, Tricks, Secrets On How To Generate A Huge Passive Income With Your Own Books Within A Short Period Of Time.

https://www.amazon.com/dp/B0CW1MJXDW

Cryptocurrency Investment Strategies: A Step By Step Guide, Tips, Tricks, Secrets And Strategies To Invest Successfully And Become A Millionaire In Cryptocurrency.

https://www.amazon.com/dp/B0D7611C9C

Design Like A Pro With Canva: The Step By Step Canva Guide To Create Professional Graphics And Transform Your Designs Instantly.

https://www.amazon.com/dp/B0D6FDQZKF

Canva Mastery For Beginners: The Complete Canva Expert Guide To Design Everything With Ease And Fast Like A Pro.

https://www.amazon.com/dp/B0D2VXN8KB

Crack Ielts Speaking Part 1: Proven Secrets, Tips and Strategies On How To Achieve An 8.0+ Band Score in Ielts Speaking Part 1 Easily.

https://www.amazon.com/dp/B0CYB14RFW

Crack Ielts Writing Task 2: Excellent Sample Answers By Topics, Tips and Strategies On How To Achieve An 8.0+ Band Score in Ielts Writing Task 2 Easily.

https://www.amazon.com/dp/B0CXJSNZSG

Ielts Speaking Part 1 By Topics: Over 200 Excellent Sample Answers By Topics You Must Know To Achieve An 8.0+ Band Score In Ielts Speaking Part 1 Easily.

https://www.amazon.com/dp/B0D2VWJHDR

Ielts Speaking Part 2 By Topics: Over 100 Excellent Sample Answers By Topics You Must Know To Achieve An 8.0+ Band Score In Ielts Speaking Part 2 Easily.

https://www.amazon.com/dp/B0D2S5ZDP6

Mastering IELTS Speaking: Achieve Band 8.0+ in Ielts Speaking with Proven Strategies, Excellent Sample Answers and Practice Exercises.

https://www.amazon.com/dp/B0CW6C9HK8

Mastering Ielts Writing: Achieve Band 8.0+ in Ielts Writing with Proven Strategies, Excellent Sample Answers and Practice Exercises.

https://www.amazon.com/dp/B0D4TD1NLC

Ielts Writing For Success: The Complete Guide To Achieve Band 8.0+ In Ielts Writing With Proven Strategies, Vocabulary & Excellent Sample Answers In 2 Weeks.

https://www.amazon.com/dp/B0D4W6JVRR

Mastering Ielts Reading: Achieve Band 8.0+ Easily in Ielts Reading with Proven Strategies, Tips, Tricks and Techniques.

https://www.amazon.com/dp/B0D2BJZBS8

www.ingramcontent.com/pod-product-compliance
Lightning Source LLC
Chambersburg PA
CBHW071836210526
45479CB00001B/168